COLLAGE

A NEW APPROACH

For
Alice Brooke McReynolds
1910-1999

COLLAGE
A NEW APPROACH

5TH EDITION

JONATHAN TALBOT

History:
First Edition — June 1998
Second Edition — August 1998
Third Edition — August 1999
Fourth Edition — February 2001
Fifth Edition — March 2001

Published by
Jonathan Talbot
7 Amity Road, Warwick, NY 10990
www.talbot1.com

Talbot, Jonathan
Collage: A New Approach, Fifth Edition / Jonathan Talbot
Includes bibliographical references, appendix, & index
ISBN 0-9701681-2-8
1. Collage— Technique 2. Artists' materials. I. Title
702'.8'12— dc20

Fifth Edition
ẽ ẽ ẽ ẽ ẽ

Third Printing — August, 2003
Printed and Bound by Royal Fireworks, Unionville, NY

Cover Art by Jonathan Talbot
Cover Design by Scott Fray and Jonathan Talbot

1 2 3 4 5 6 7

CONTENTS

Introduction   1

Overview of the Process   5

Details of the Basic Process   8

Polyvinyl Acetate Adhesive   17

Acrylic Image Transfers   19

Additional Techniques   23

Adhesives and their Alternatives   27

Varnishing   30

Presentation   33

Archival Concerns   37

Appendix   46

Index   54

COLLAGE: A NEW APPROACH

PART I

INTRODUCTION

This book has been written for beginning and experienced artists alike. Mindful of the difficulties which I encountered while developing the techniques and concepts which are the subjects of this volume, I have proceeded on the assumption that including a little too much in these pages will be far better than leaving out something of importance to even one reader. Thanks to modern computer technology, this book is a work-in-progress and subject to continual revision. I hope you will contact me with your suggestions for improvement. — JT

Defining "Collage." — The word collage is derived from the French *coller*, to paste or glue. The word collage, therefore, has come to mean a work of art in which there are pasted or glued elements. Many artists combine collage with other media and call the resulting works "collages."

Collage differs from assemblage or construction in that collages are basically flat while assemblage and construction are primarily three-dimensional. Many collages, however, do include three-dimensional elements and we are, as artists, well-advised to remember that we have the privilege of defining our work in any way which delights us.

Paper, fabric, metal leaf, flower petals, foil, bark, and paint are just some of the materials which find their way into collages.

The advent of computers has put new and powerful tools into the hands of today's artists. Not only can one create entire images on a computer screen, one can also use today's sophisticated software to "manufacture" custom-made elements for insertion into hand-made collages. The definitions associated with digital collage are still evolving and it is premature to codify them at this point. Again, each artist has the right, and perhaps the responsibility, to define his or her work as he or she sees fit.

History of Collage.[1] — While the history of making or assembling images (both representational and abstract) from applied materials goes back centuries, it is currently common to credit Picasso with having created the first "modern" collage when he included a piece of printed oil cloth in his work *Still Life with Chair Caning* (1911-12). Perhaps because of Picasso's preeminence in the world of art during the second decade of the 20th century, collage "caught on" quickly. The years 1912 - 1920 saw the creation of many works with collaged elements. Among the early 20th century explorers of collage was Picasso's studio-mate Georges Braque and Jean Arp, Juan Gris, Umberto Boccioni, Francis Picabia, Gino Severini, Kasimir Malevich, and Man Ray.

Since that time many artists have created wonderful collage works. Among the better known are Max Ernst,

---

[1] A monograph of this scope can do little more than list a few names. The reader is encouraged to seek out and experience these artists' works in galleries, museums, and books containing reproductions of their works.

George Grosz, Hannah Höch, Marcel Duchamp, Arthur G. Dove, Joan Miró, and Henri Matisse. Kurt Schwitters and Romare Bearden chose collage as their primary medium and Joseph Cornell combined it with assemblage to make works of remarkable insight. More recently Alberto Burri, Mimmo Rotella, Robert Motherwell, Robert Rauschenberg, Fred Otnes, Robert Ohnigian, Friedrich Meckseper, and David Hockney have contributed to the body of exceptional collage works which are widely reproduced.

Among the new contributors to the canon of collage Nick Bantock, Laura Breitman, Nessa Grainger, Claudine Hellmuth, Gennielynn Martin, Maureen McCabe, Roderick Slater, and Peter Tytla are among those who have created works which inspire and inform their audiences.

The Potential of Collage.— In addition to having aesthetic qualities such as hue, value, chroma, texture, shape, etc., "found" collage materials are often highly charged with personal, social, political, economic, philosophic, or other implications. Collages, therefore, in addition to being physically layered, are often emotionally, historically, spiritually, and mythically layered as well. This increases the potential of the collage experience for both artists and their audiences.

Compositional Opportunities.— Unlike painting or drawing, collage offers the artist the opportunity to easily add and remove, and to arrange and rearrange, the elements of his or her work in an effort to arrive at the best possible composition. This makes collage an ideal medium for exploring new ideas.

Safety. — Most of the materials and tools discussed in this book are among the safer and more benign available to the artist. Toxic substances have, however, found their way into all aspects of our lives and as a result warnings on product manufacturers' labels should be heeded and common sense exercised as well.

About the Techniques in this Book.— Some would maintain that it is necessary to unlearn old patterns in order to learn new ones. At times that may be true, but it is the author's hope that the techniques described here will become additions to, rather than replacements for, the artist-reader's existing repertoire of familiar, successful techniques.

☙

PART II

OVERVIEW OF THE PROCESS

It was impatience and dissatisfaction rather than necessity which inspired the development of the techniques which are outlined in these pages. However, now that these techniques are part of my creative life, I would be lost without them. — JT

One of the joys of collage is that it allows the artist to visually explore a variety of compositional opportunities. By moving, adjusting, adding, replacing, and removing loose collage elements the artist can experience a variety of compositions until a satisfactory arrangement is achieved. A frequent source of frustration, however, is the necessity of *disassembling* compositions in order to apply adhesive and glue the elements in place. Not only is this extra work, but all too often it is impossible to successfully recreate your original arrangement. The technique outlined in these pages makes it possible to adhere collage elements without disassembly. By removing liquid adhesives from the collage assembly process, wrinkling and drying time are also eliminated, offering new opportunities for creative spontaneity.

This technique requires that the materials which will be used in a collage be pre-coated with acrylic medium which is allowed to dry before work on the collage begins. The compositional elements are then cut, torn, manipulated, or otherwise arranged until a satisfactory arrangement has been achieved. The elements are then adhered with heat which reactivates the adhesive qualities of the acrylic medium. This technique and variations of it work with paper, fabric, foil, string, and other materials.

The pictures and captions which follow provide a brief overview of the process. A few of the tools and materials used may be unfamiliar to some readers. They will be explained in the pages which follow.

Preparing the Substrate - The first step is to coat the substrate (support) with gloss acrylic medium. Often the surface is toned with a neutral value acrylic paint (with or without the addition of colored pencil or other media) before applying the pure gloss medium. In this photo, all-rag matboard is being used as a substrate.

Preparing the Materials - The second step is to coat both sides of all anticipated (some may end up not being used) materials (found or painted papers, fabrics, etc.) with gloss acrylic medium. Normally one side is "painted" with medium, that side is allowed to dry, and then the other side is "painted". Sometimes materials are hung up to dry as shown here. They can also be dried horizontally on wire racks made from the fine wire hexagonal mesh screening known as "poultry mesh", stretched on wooden frames.

Creating the Composition- The pre-coated materials are then cut or torn into the desired shapes and arranged into a composition. As the composition develops, the sizes and shapes of the elements of the composition may be altered by cutting or tearing or they may be discarded or replaced.

Adhering the Elements- When the composition has been achieved, the elements are covered with release paper and, a tacking iron is used to apply pressure and heat which causes the acrylic coating on the surface of the elements to fuse with the acrylic coating on the substrate.

Notes:

Release Paper: Release paper is paper impregnated and coated with silicone. Almost nothing sticks to release paper. If release paper were not used between the iron and the collage elements, the elements would stick to the iron and char. (see *Appendix: Release Paper*)

Tacking Iron: A tacking iron is a small version of a household iron. In theory, you could use a household iron, but in fact, when using a household iron the heat is dispersed over too broad an area to be useful (except when ironing-down large sheets of paper in larger collages). (see *Appendix: Tacking Irons*)

PART III

DETAILS OF THE BASIC PROCESS

The following paragraphs discuss the basic process in detail. There are a number of variations on this process each of which has unique advantages and each of which will be explained in turn. It is in our best interest to proceed with an examination of the basic process before examining the variations. — JT

Preparing the Substrate. — Among the materials available as substrates for collages four stand out: all-rag matboard, watercolor paper, braced wooden panels and canvas. Other supports may be used but for the sake of brevity this discussion will focus on these four.

Matboard as a Substrate. — Matboard is suitable for collages up to 24" x 36" in size. When using matboard, 100% cotton neutral pH museum board (also called "all rag" matboard) is desirable since the chemical sizing in regular paper matboard will cause it to self-destruct in just a few decades. Acid-free matboard which is not 100% cotton may be an acceptable substitute. It will certainly last longer than regular paper mat which is acidic beer-coaster material with a sheet of paper glued to each side.

It is a good idea to work on a piece of matboard which is larger than the intended size of the final collage. Matboard edges dent easily during handling and a collage on matboard can easily be trimmed after it is finished (or almost finished– see Part IX).

Toning the Surface. — Toning the surface of the white museum board with paint (acrylic or watercolor) or with colored pencils, or almost any other non-oil medium provides a more-or-less neutral ground similar to that used by classical painters. If the ground is white, one can only delineate images with darker lines (and vice versa) but if the ground is neutral it is possible to use both light and dark strokes to define a composition.

Coating the Matboard. — It is necessary to coat the front of the matboard with acrylic medium to prepare it for receiving the collage elements. When the front has dried, it is a good idea to also coat the back. Coating both sides equalizes the stress on the flexible board and inhibits warping.[2] Sometimes, if the matboard and/or its painted coating has absorbed too much of the medium, a second coat is necessary. Make your determination based on the sheen of the surface. The ironing-down technique described in this monograph works best when both surfaces have a dry but glossy coating of acrylic medium.

When using matboard, keep in mind that when your composition is finished you may want to trim the edges and mount it on a sheet of paper or mat over the edges when the work is framed. Both approaches offer the opportunity to trim off (or mat out) various parts of the work in order to enhance the final composition.

Watercolor Paper as a Substrate. — Watercolor paper is a suitable support for collages of almost any size up to 22" x 30". When using watercolor paper, take into consideration that when framing the finished work you may want to float the sheet in a recessed mat (see Part IX). Some artists work from edge to edge of the watercolor paper. Others prefer clean margins around the image. You can protect

---

[2] The matboard can also be stapled to a piece of masonite or plywood in order to keep it flat or it may be permanently laminated to a stiffer support such as plywood, gatorboard, or sintra (this latter approach can make framing difficult)..

the margins of your paper while you create your collage by using 3M (Scotch brand) Safe Release Masking Tape #2070.[3] Cover the edges of the sheet of watercolor paper with this newly-developed tape before you start work. This tape is so low-tack that it will not damage even delicate papers.[4]

Having defined your margins with this tape, tone the exposed "image area" (see previous section) and then coat it with gloss acrylic medium. If you find that the paper warps as a result of this coating apply a coating of acrylic medium to the back of the paper as well. It is acceptable to stop before reaching the edges of the back of the sheet in order to ensure that the edges stay clean.

Choosing watercolor paper as a substrate eliminates the necessity of mounting your matboard-based collage on a separate sheet of paper.

Prepared Panels as Substrates. — Braced wooden panels also make good supports for larger collages (there is no limit to the size of the work you can make on a carefully constructed and prepared panel). Braced panels are most often made from plywood reinforced by the addition of a wooden grid attached to the back.

Hollow Core Doors.[5] — For collages under 3 x 6½ feet in size, hollow core doors (which are available at most lumber yards) are a less expensive and remarkably stable substitute for custom made braced panels. Hollow core doors are available from 12" to 36" in width and normally

---

[3] This tape is not distributed as widely to art stores as one might expect. For additional information and sources see *Appendix: Masking Tapes.*

[4] You must be careful because it does not adhere as strongly as normal masking tape and casually applied paint or medium may seep under the edge.

[5] Recently (2000), the manufacturers of hollow core doors have replaced the wood facing with a laminate of cardboard and a very thin veneer of wood. This makes newer hollow core doors less desirable as substrates.

measure 80" or so in height. On special order you can also purchase hollow core doors up to 48" wide.[6]

Hollow core doors are not truly hollow as they are made with a grid of support which prevents them from warping. You can "cut down" hollow core doors with a hand-held circular saw (using all necessary safety equipment and taking all precautions) fitted with a fine-toothed plywood blade. You will then need to fill the open "hollow" end which results with a piece of wood carefully cut to size.

Whether braced panels or hollow core doors are used, you should prime the raw wood with acrylic gesso or some other sealer before coating the surface with gloss medium to prepare it to accept collage elements.

Canvas as a Substrate. — Canvas can also be a suitable support for collages of almost any size. Canvas must also be primed and coated with enough acrylic medium to provide a glossy, receptive surface for the "ironing-down" process. If you are using canvas on a stretcher, it will be necessary to build a temporary support which is the same thickness as the stretcher to provide a solid backing for the canvas while you are ironing collage elements down.

Figure 3-1

When using canvas, especially canvas which has not been stretched, you should handle your collage carefully as the canvas may be more flexible than the collage elements which have been adhered to the surface and thus the

---

[6] Birch-faced doors, while slightly more expensive, are better than those faced with mahogany.

elements may crack or tear if the canvas is bent or rolled too tightly.

Preparing the Materials. — Preparing the materials requires coating them on both sides with gloss acrylic medium. It is most efficient to coat entire sheets of paper and cut or tear them up afterwards. Coating before cutting also yields better results as the medium tends to "bead up" along the edges of materials during the coating process and if you cut after the coating is dry you will be able to trim that beading away.

To coat sheets of paper or fabric, lay them on a clean piece of paper (newsprint works well) and brush on the medium with a conveniently wide brush. Try to get as even a coating as possible since lumps and ridges may prove to be unsightly or even structurally problematic later on, but do not dilute the medium as this will adversely effect its thermoplastic qualities. Once a sheet or piece has been coated, do not allow it to remain on the newsprint for the coated piece may stick where your brush has passed over the edges. Either hang it up to dry *(see illustrations in Part II)* or move it to some sort of low-contact drying rack.[7]

It is normally best to coat the side which you intend to be the "front" or "face" first. After coating the front, lay the freshly coated paper face up on your drying racks until the medium is dry. Then remove the paper from the drying rack, coat the back, and replace on the drying rack until dry. It is important to have a clean sheet of paper under each piece each time you apply a new coating. You can do this by placing a newspaper on your worktable, opening it to the first interior page, coating a sheet of material, and then turning to the next page of the

---

[7] Racks made of poultry mesh stretched over wooden frames are excellent for drying coated materials as the paper makes only minimal contact with the mesh, especially if it is mesh with wider openings (2" or more).

newspaper before going on to the next sheet to be coated. This ensures an orderly supply of clean, dry pages.

In the case of extremely thick or porous materials, it is often necessary to apply two coats of gloss medium to each side, judging whether or not this is required by the degree of glossiness of the surface. A glossy surface will adhere better than one which is somewhat dull. A little experimentation will give you a sense of how many coats of medium are required for different kinds of paper. [8]

After coating the materials allow them to dry thoroughly.

Storing Prepared Materials — In order to make sure that coated materials (see pages 6 & 12) do not stick to each other if stacked and stored while waiting to be made into collages, it is best to store them with dry uncoated pieces of paper between each pair of coated pieces. This is especially important if the conditions are hot or damp. Sheets of inexpensive copy machine paper serve well for this purpose.

Author's Note:

I have often been asked whether matte medium will work for coating the materials. Matte medium will work for this technique but not nearly as well, in my experience, as gloss medium. I have also been asked whether one can use any brand of gloss medium. I have tried a number of different mediums and they vary somewhat in the degree of adhesion which can be achieved. I recommend the gloss medium made by Golden Artist Colors, a forward looking company whose high-quality products are increasingly widely distributed.

---

[8]Preliminary preparation of the materials may involve painting them or tinting them with washes or glazes of various colors. When this is done it is important that such painting or tinting be done prior to the application of the gloss medium or, if the painting or tinting is an afterthought, that an additional final coat of gloss medium be applied following the application of color.

Creating the Composition.[9] — After the coated papers, fabrics, etc. have been allowed to dry thoroughly, you can cut (with scissors, knives, paper cutters, special scissors like pinking shears, circle cutters, etc.) tear, rip (papers or fabrics), or use whole, any of the coated materials. You can arrange as many elements as you like and, since they are dry, move and remove them at will until a satisfactory composition has been achieved. You can then adhere all the elements to the substrate without disassembling the composition as outlined below.

Adhering the Elements. — The elements are adhered by ironing them together. Two surfaces coated with acrylic gloss medium will "fuse" or melt together when heated. This method provides an extremely strong and permanent bond.[10] It is important to find the right source of heat and to protect the materials from fusing with the heat source. These points are covered in the next two sections: "The Tacking Iron" and "Release paper."

The Tacking Iron. — A tacking iron (shown at right) provides a localized and adjustable source of heat which can be applied

Figure 3-2

to whole elements or just parts of them (more about this later). Not only can you apply heat with the tacking iron, you can also apply gentle pressure at the same time and this combination is what works best.

The reader is encouraged to use a tacking iron which has a variable temperature control. Success with a wide variety of different materials will be enhanced by the ability to

---

[9] Since this short work focuses on technical issues, discussion of composition and visual linguistics has been deemed outside its scope. The author hopes to examine these subjects in a future work.

[10] Under some circumstances this bond is reversible with heat (See *Part VI - Removal of Elements*)

control the temperature of the iron. In general, setting your iron to 225° Fahrenheit is a good place to start. Thicker or heavier papers or fabrics will require higher temperatures and thinner materials sometimes work best with lower temperatures. The exact temperature required depends not only on the thickness of the material but also on how long you allow the iron to "dwell" in one position ("dwell time") before moving on. When using irons with uncalibrated temperature controls (temperature controls with just "low, medium, and high" settings) it is best to start with the iron set at "medium" and adjust up or down based on your experience.[11]

Release Paper. — The tacking iron cannot be applied directly to the materials you wish to adhere because a) the faces of those materials are covered with medium which would melt and stick to the iron and b) even if there were no acrylic medium on the face of the papers and fabrics you are adhering, the iron would be likely to smear the inks or varnishes which are to be found on many "found" papers or otherwise damage the materials. You should, therefore, place a sheet of release paper between the iron and the materials you are adhering.

Release paper is paper which has been impregnated and coated with silicone in order to provide a non-stick surface not unlike the Teflon or Silverstone coating on many modern cooking utensils. Release paper is used behind self adhesive labels and postage stamps and during the drymounting process in frame shops.

In order to prevent damage to the surface of papers or fabrics which have been coated with acrylic medium while adhering them to a medium-coated substrate by means of heat, you should always place a sheet of release paper

---

[11] For additional information on Tacking Irons see *Appendix: Tacking Irons*

between the tacking iron and whatever you are "ironing down."

Most release paper has non-stick coating on both sides. There are a few sources, however, which sell single-sided release paper. It is better to find the double-sided kind as that way mistakes are less likely. The release paper can be used over and over again. While the silicone surface of the release paper eventually "wears out," you can often make six or more small collages, or one large one, using the same sheet of release paper. It is a good idea to always place the same side of the sheet of release paper that you are using against the work for after some use the iron will soil the other side and the marks of the iron can be transferred to the work if the soiled side of the release paper is faced in that direction.

Tissue Paper and Other Exceptions. — There are a number of materials which are not amenable to, or do not require, precoating. Among them are tissue paper, silk (and similar synthetic fabrics), feathers, some flower petals, metal leaf, hot stamping foils, and thread. Most of these materials, too fragile to allow the brushing on of medium, may be ironed down without any precoating as long as the receiving surface has been coated with an ample layer of medium. *(For more information on these exceptions see Part VI.)*

REVIEW

The basic steps of the gloss acrylic medium adhesion process are:
1. Coat the surface with gloss acrylic medium and allow to dry.
2. Coat the elements with gloss acrylic medium and allow to dry.
3. Adhere the elements by applying heat.

PART IV

SUBSTITUTING POLYVINYL ACETATE ADHESIVE FOR ACRYLIC MEDIUM

Artists wishing to preserve the natural surfaces and textures of their materials and still enjoy the convenience and advantages of "ironing" collages together may wish to substitute polyvinyl acetate adhesive (PVA) for gloss acrylic medium.

Different PVA adhesives have different qualities. Among the archival PVA adhesives which I have tried, Lineco® Neutral pH Polyvinyl Acetate (PVA) Adhesive works well for ironing on collage elements. It's transparent matte finish is so clear and dull that even if it gets on the front of one of your collage elements, you can hardly see it. USArtQuest's Perfect Paper Adhesive™ Gloss (an acrylic adhesive, not a PVA adhesive) also works well for ironing on but requires care in application to make sure it does not get on the face of elements where its gloss finish may not be desired.[12]

When substituting polyvinyl acetate adhesive for gloss acrylic medium, apply a liberal but even (in thickness) coat of the PVA adhesive to the back of the elements you are going to use. It is not necessary to apply adhesive to the front of the materials when using PVA Adhesive. Allow the elements to dry and then arrange them as desired on top of all-rag matboard or watercolor paper.

---

[12] Collage elements ironed down with regular (non-gloss) Perfect Paper Adhesive™ did not adhere well. —JT (See *Appendix: PVA Adhesives* for additional information)

To adhere the elements, cover them with release paper, apply heat with the tacking iron.

It is important to note that it is not necessary to coat the substrate when ironing on with PVA adhesive. This allows the artist to preserve the natural surface of collage elements. It also facilitates the creation of collages with irregular borders on uncoated substrates, a technique especially suited to working on watercolor paper.

The effectiveness of this method depends, to some extent, on the degree to which the material being adhered absorbs the PVA adhesive when it is applied. With absorbent materials you may have to apply two or more coats of adhesive in order to insure a good bond. It is desirable to be able to see the coating of PVA adhesive on the surface of the material before attempting to iron it down.

PART V

ACRYLIC IMAGE TRANSFERS

Sometimes it is desirable to insert type or a found or drawn image into a work without "covering up" the background with paper. One way of doing this also utilizes gloss acrylic medium.[13] Use of the proper paper in combination with gloss acrylic medium will allow the "paperless" transfer of printed or photocopied images.

To transfer an image using gloss acrylic medium follow these steps:

1. Create image on Image Transfer Paper. This may be done by printing, photocopying, laser printer output, or by drawing with *waterproof* ink.
2. Cover the face of the image with gloss acrylic medium. Do *not* cover back of image transfer paper.
3. Allow to dry.
4. Coat the surface which is to receive the image with gloss acrylic medium.
5. Allow receiving surface to dry also.
6. Iron image *face-down* onto receiving surface.
7. Wash away Transfer Paper by rubbing with water and woven cotton cloth (a scrap of old bed sheet works well).

You should end up with the type or image you wished to transfer affixed to receiving surface without obscuring the

---

[13] Another transfer method (Rauschenberg's *Dante's Inferno* series is an example) involves saturating printed images with solvents (benzine or toluene, among others) and then rubbing the backs of the images to transfer the ink to the "receiving" surface. Unlike gloss acrylic medium, these solvents are highly flammable, give off toxic fumes which are reported to be carcinogenic, and are, therefore, not recommended.

surrounding background. The following pictures help describe the process.

Figure 5-1
The image to be transferred. It's face (but not its back) has been coated with gloss acrylic medium.

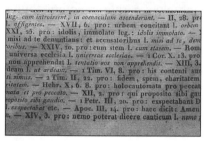

Figure 5-2
The receiving surface. It has also been coated with gloss acrylic medium.

Figure 5-3
After the "transfer" has been "ironed on" face down, the transfer paper is "washed" or "rubbed" away with a cloth, saturated with water, wrapped around finger tip.

Figure 5-4
The transferred image in place on the receiving surface. No transfer paper remains and the background "shows through" the transferred image.

Why this Process Works. — This process works because image transfer paper is clay coated unvarnished paper and acrylic medium will adhere to the top layer of the clay coating but will not penetrate it to reach the fibers of the paper. Thus the "body" of the paper itself can be washed away. Happily, acrylic medium renders the clay coating transparent so only the printed or photocopied images remain.

Some periodicals are printed on clay coated unvarnished paper. That means that you can transfer type and/or images directly from those periodicals.[14] Among such publications are Time, Newsweek, and Scientific American. Only the interior pages will work. The covers are printed and varnished. Newspapers will not work (they have no clay coating) and glossy pages like those in Smithsonian or National Geographic will not work because they are varnished.

Notes:

1. Transferred images or type will be reversed. If it is important to retain the original orientation of the image, the image must be created with a Canon color copier or other machine (laser printer) and created in a program (Quark or Pagemaker) which will create a reverse or mirror image. Such images, when transferred, regain their original orientation. Another way of retaining orientation is to photocopy the image onto transparent film, invert the film, and recopy onto transfer paper.

2. This method will not work with some water-based inks as the images will smear during the coating procedure.

---

[14] Since such periodicals are copyrighted you must, if you wish to remain within the law, obtain permission before using the images.

3. Canon and other color copies are subject to fading. Black copies, including those made on Canon color copiers, will not fade.

4. When rubbing with the moistened cloth it is helpful to rub from the center of the transfer towards the edges in order to avoid inadvertently lifting an edge.

5. Gloss Acrylic Medium is the suggested adhesive for transfers. Some PVA adhesives are redissolvable in water and will not work at all.

Alternative Acrylic Medium Transfer Methods. — The first of the following methods works only with photocopies. The second will work with other kinds of images.

Method 1. Make a photocopy of the image you wish to transfer. Place the image face down on a receiving surface coated with gloss acrylic medium. Rub the back of the photocopy with a heated tool such as a tacking iron. The toner which makes up the image should melt and transfer to the receiving surface.[15]

Method 2. Repeatedly coat images on clay coated paper with enough coats of *gel* acrylic medium to build up a film which is substantial enough to allow the paper to be washed away *before* the image is placed on a supporting surface. The film, with the image on it, can then be glued or ironed into position. *Note: This method leaves a ridge at the edge of the film (because of its thickness).*

---

[15] Care should be exercised not to exert too much pressure which may cause the paper itself to adhere.

PART VI

ADDITIONAL TECHNIQUES

In addition to eliminating the need for disassembly, the wrinkling caused by wet adhesives, and extended drying time, the ironing-on of precoated collage elements offers a variety of additional advantages.

Removal of Elements. — Sometimes elements can be removed by reversing the adhesion process. This is especially effective when an element has not been ironed down in its entirety. To remove an "ironed-down" element lift one corner (use a blade and tweezers if necessary) and, placing release paper over the element, gently heat it with the tacking iron to soften the medium. As the medium softens, tug gently and lift the corner, backing the tacking iron away as you do so. With luck[16] and practice you will be able to remove the element.

Gilding. — Metal Leaf (gold or silver, genuine or imitation) may be ironed directly onto a surface coated with acrylic medium without the use of any additional size[17] as long as release paper is used. A little experimentation will reveal the advantages of this option.

Feathers, Silk, and Other Fragile or Thin Materials. — Some materials do not need to be precoated in order to be ironed-down. These are usually thin or fragile materials like feathers, silk, dried flower petals, thread, etc. If the receiving surface has one or two good coats of gloss acrylic the heat from the tacking iron is usually sufficient to embed enough of these thin materials into the medium

---

[16] Type of paper, amount of medium originally used, and amount of pressure originally used all play a role in determining the outcome.

[17] *size* is the normal adhesive for metal leaf

to cause them to adhere. Don't forget to cover the materials with release paper before ironing them down.

Registration / Exact Abutment. — Sometimes it may be desirable to have two paper elements fit together exactly without overlapping. It is possible to do this with great precision by adhering the pieces to the substrate without ironing down those parts which touch. This allows the artist to cut through both pieces with a single knife cut, insuring that the pieces will meet exactly. After removing the excess material the ironing-down process is completed.

Figure 6-1

Two elements are partially adhered to the surface. Only the circled areas have been ironed down.

Figure 6-2

A single cut is made with a knife through both elements.

Figure 6-3

The excess material is removed and the ironing-down completed. The two elements meet exactly.

Hot Stamping Foil. — Hot stamping foil is an ultra-thin layer of metal attached to a plastic backing. When the metal side is pressed against a surface and heated, the metal will stick to the surface and the plastic can be peeled away. Rolls of used hot stamping foil (used for stamping leather goods, book covers, etc.)[18] often contain "negative" or "reverse" images which can be easily transferred to surfaces coated with gloss acrylic medium even without the use of release paper. You need only apply the iron to the glossy (plastic) side of the foil. Hot stamping foil also works well when shapes are cut out and ironed down (you must use release paper for this, and you must remember to peel away the plastic backing) or when free form areas are applied by using the tacking iron as a drawing or painting tool. Hot stamping foil is available in a variety of metallic finishes and a variety of colors as well.[19]

Cutting Circles. — Cutting circles is made much easier if you acquire a drafting compass of the kind which is normally made to accept a pencil lead (not the kind which holds a complete pencil but the kind that holds just the slim graphite rod). The plastic shaft of X-Acto's No. 9RX blade has a diameter close to that of a pencil lead and so you can substitute this extremely sharp blade for the lead in appropriate compasses.[20] Orient the axis of the blade perpendicular to the line drawn between the two points of

---

[18] This material is usually discarded (except when genuine gold is used) by the metal foil stampers. Check the yellow pages for Hot Foil Stamping and hopefully you will find a free source.

[19] Unused sheets of heat-transferable foil may be obtained under a variety of brand names in stationery or art stores. They are used for drawing (with a heated point) or for ironing onto the toner of photocopies (the toner melts under the heat and the foil adheres).

[20] Sometimes you need to remove the round "mushroom" head at the end of this blade in order to make it fit into the compass. Use a pair of wire-cutting pliers. Caution: this blade is very sharp– handle with care.

the compass. Larger circles may require a beam compass. The 9RX blade will fit in many of these as well.

Drawing Lines. — There are a number of ways to insert linear elements into collages. Thread and string work well (thread need not be pre-coated as it will embed itself in an acrylic medium surface when ironed down). Thin strips of paper also can provide linear elements. Still, sometimes you may wish to draw lines and in that case an "old-fashioned" ruling pen (sometimes called a drafting pen) can be very useful.[21]

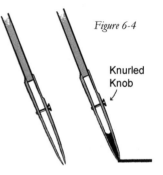

Figure 6-4

Knurled Knob

Ruling pens are no longer as common as they once were (they have been replaced by rapidographs and computers). Their writing end is adjustable, opening and closing like the beak of a bird by means of a knurled knob. Ruling pens will work just as well with paint as they will with ink, thus offering the artist a variety of permanent colors. By loading the reservoir with diluted paint and adjusting the width of the opening by means of the knurled knob you can make straight or free-form lines in a variety of widths. Why do ruling pens work? Surface tension keeps the liquid from flowing out of the opening until it contacts the surface *(see Figure 6-4)*.

❧

---

[21] Ruling pens work well with acrylics, oils and watercolors and, with a little practice, make an ideal tool for signing paintings as well as collages. (See *Appendix: Ruling Pens*)

PART VII

ADHESIVES AND THEIR ALTERNATIVES

Reasons for Using a Variety of Adhesives. — No single technique or material is ideal in all circumstances. Each artist should be prepared to use whatever best serves her or his needs *and* the needs of the work being made. The "ironing-on" technique described in this book offers advantages in many situations (especially those where the collage materials are relatively thin), but there are circumstances where other methods and adhesives are preferable.

Stable Adhesives. — Some adhesives are longer lasting than others. Acrylic Medium, Neutral pH Polyvinyl Acetate Adhesives, Elmer's® Glue, and Wheat Paste[22] are among the more stable. These adhesives undergo minimal alteration as time passes and are not likely to discolor and alter the appearance of your collage.

Adhesives to Avoid. — There are some common adhesives which the artist who wishes to make long lasting work does well to avoid. Among them are Rubber Cement and Model Adhesive (the kind used for assembling wooden and plastic models). Rubber Cement turns brown and penetrates the papers which it touches,

---

[22] Wheat paste, a simple mixture of flour and water, has been used for centuries to adhere paper. Over time, the starches in wheat paste can change to sugar and attract insects or grow mold. Some conservators add a small amount of *thymol* (the chemical that gives Listerine its unique smell and taste) to their wheat paste to avoid such problems. The artist who chooses to do this should do so with extreme caution since concentrated *thymol* is a poison.

staining them severely. Model Adhesive also darkens and stains the materials which it touches.

Three-Dimensional Elements. — Selecting the proper adhesive for attaching three dimensional elements depends on what those elements are made of. The following table may prove helpful in making a selection.

Adhesive	Paper	Wood	Ceramic	Plastic[1]	Glass	Metal	Fabric	Archival	Stains or Discolors
Acrylic Medium	×						×	Y	N
PVA (Neutral pH)	×	×					×	Y	N
Elmer's	×	×					×	?	?
Yes Glue[2]	×							N	?
Rubber Cement[3]	×							N	Y
Epoxy[4]	×	×	×	×	×	×	×	N	Y
Model Adhesive[5]	×	×	×	×		×	×	N	Y
Crazy Glue	Not Recommended because of Danger								
Hot Glue Gun	Not Recommended because of Danger								

[1] Some plastics reject all adhesives [2] Contains compounds which turn to sugar
[3] Darkens & bleeds through paper [4] Darkens with time [5] Use with adequate ventilation

Epoxy. — Epoxy is a good adhesive for attaching three dimensional items to collages. Epoxy sticks to almost everything[23]. No pressure is needed as epoxy will even form a "bridge" between two elements which do not touch.

Epoxy comes in two separate containers. Equal amounts (but not necessarily all) of the contents of both containers must be mixed immediately before use. Unlike any of the other adhesives mentioned here, epoxy does not depend on exposure to air in order to dry. Instead, it cures as a result of the chemical reaction between its two components. For this reason it is important that the two

---

[23] Some plastics reject all adhesives

components remain uncontaminated by each other since the slightest amount of one will cause the other to solidify.

One easy way to mix epoxy is to squeeze out two parallel strips of the two components on a piece of cardboard or paper and then mix them with a popsicle stick or similar piece of wood. It is particularly effective to alternately spread the mixture in one direction and then "scrape it up" in a direction perpendicular to the spreading. Mixing in this manner is much more effective than a circular stirring motion.

Epoxy must be used soon after it is mixed. With some brands one has only five minutes before the adhesive begins to harden. Other brands have a longer working time.

Epoxy darkens with time so one must be careful to make sure that it is hidden by the objects fastened with it. It is not suggested for use in fastening transparent objects.

Alternatives to Adhesives. — There are many ways of attaching elements to your collage, especially three-dimensional elements. Fabric and leather may be *sewn* to a substrate. Buttons, feathers, and other objects may be *tied* in place. Wood objects may be *screwed* or *nailed* from the front or back of the work. Metal and plastic objects may be fastened with *bolts and nuts* or *tied* to a surface (sometimes it will be necessary to drill or poke holes in the substrate). Sometimes *a group of elements* can be used to *hold another element in place* much as paper corners were used to hold photographs in place in old photograph albums.

❧

PART VIII

VARNISHING COLLAGES

Reasons for Varnishing Collages. — Upon completing your collage it is a good idea to varnish it. Among the reasons for this are 1) Proper varnish will help insure stability and permanency and, if the varnish is removable, will allow the work to be cleaned in the future, 2) A choice of matte, satin, or gloss varnishes can produce the desired surface appearance, and 3) A coat of varnish can "even out" the reflective irregularities created during the construction of the work.

Understanding Varnishes. — Varnishes are not mediums. Although formulated to be flexible and forgiving, they tend to be harder than mediums,[24] thus preventing dust and dirt from adhering to the work as time passes.

It is desirable to use a varnish which can be removed by an agent other than that which will dissolve the medium which has been used to create your work. This is important because it may become necessary, at some future date, to remove the varnish in order to clean the work.[25]

---

[24] This hardness can be problematic if the varnish is not also flexible. Varnish which is too hard can crack when the softer medium beneath it expands and contracts.

[25] The makers of one brand of acrylic gloss medium label their product "Acrylic Medium and Varnish". It is important to avoid using this product as both medium and varnish since it will be difficult or

Some varnishes can, in addition to protecting the work from dirt and dust, also reduce the possibility of fading of "found" materials. This is a particular benefit to collage artists because many "found" materials used in collages are printed with inks which are not lightfast. A number of new varnishes (including Golden's water-soluble *Polymer Varnish with UVLS*) contain materials which filter out ultraviolet light, the light which is most likely to cause fading and paper discoloration. These varnishes act like a clear "sunscreen," preventing fading in the same way that sunscreen prevents sunburn during a day at the beach. [26]

When to Varnish. — Do not varnish your work until it is complete. Although you may be able to apply acrylic medium over acrylic varnish, in the long term doing so will make the layers of your collage unstable. It is better to be sure that your work is finished before you apply varnish.

Isolation Coat. — Before varnishing your collage apply a coat or two of undiluted gloss medium to the finished work to seal the surface.

Varnishing Collages with Water Soluble Varnishes. — If you select a water-based acrylic varnish, apply the varnish with a soft brush which has been thoroughly cleaned in water. One inch wide soft white nylon watercolor brushes are good for small collages. Use long gentle strokes. The folks at Golden suggest that their varnishes containing ultraviolet light screen be thinned with water, 1 part water to three parts varnish. Try it thinned and unthinned and make your own choice.

Varnishing Collages with Mineral Spirits Soluble Varnishes. — If you select a mineral spirits (turpentine or

---

impossible to remove the varnish coat without damaging the integrity of the work itself.

[26] For additional important information on varnishes see *Appendix: Varnishes.*

paint thinner are examples) based varnish, you will need adequate ventilation to avoid the dangers of breathing the fumes. Keep in mind that some traditional artist's varnishes (damar, for example) yellow with time. For this reason some of the new synthetic varnishes are more desirable. Also, some of the new synthetic varnishes also contain ultraviolet light inhibitors. You will need a soft brush and you will need to clean it promptly after applying the varnish if you wish to reuse it. You can thin these varnishes with mineral spirits if you like. Again, try it thinned and unthinned and use your own judgment.

Protection other than Varnish. — For those artists who prefer not to varnish their works a possible source of protection is framing the work under glass (or plastic). If done correctly, this will effectively keep dirt away from the work. [27]

---

[27] See *"Glazing"* in the *Appendix* for more information on this subject.

PART IX

PRESENTATION:
TRIMMING, MOUNTING, MATTING & GLAZING

Collages on Matboard Substrates. — Collages made on matboard may be presented in a variety of ways. Some artists like to cover the edges of their collages with a mat. Others like to float their collages (leave the edges of the image showing) in a mat opening. I like to "mount" my collages on sheets of heavy all-rag paper and then float the result against a white back-ground in the opening of an extra thick white mat as shown at right. This approach provides me with a border in which to title and sign my works and makes an elegant presentation.

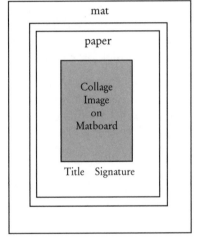

Figure 9-1

Collages made on matboard substrates may be trimmed when the composition is complete or nearly complete. A beveled edge looks nice and may be achieved by trimming with a mat cutter. It is important, if you intend to trim your collage in this fashion, to do so before significant three-dimensional elements are added as they may make cutting with a mat cutter difficult.

When mounting collages made on matboard onto their paper backings first determine the final position of the collage image by carefully measuring the margins. Once this has been done place a clean carpenter's square on one corner of the collage to mark the position. Then remove the matboard image and, using the same PVA adhesive which was described in Part IV, apply enough to effectively glue the matboard to the paper backing but not so much that it will squeeze out around the edges when the image is placed in position. Place the collage image back in the position indicated by the carpenter's square, remove the square, cover the image with plastic kitchen wrap, and apply weight. The plastic wrap diminishes the possibility of the weights sticking to or damaging the surface of the work.

Sometimes, despite your best efforts, a little of the glue does ooze out and bead up at the edge of the collage. When this happens, allow the glue to get "leather hard" and then pick off the beads with a sharp blade.

Tearing Paper.— Whether you are mounting your collages on paper or creating them directly on paper, the result will be enhanced if the edges of the paper are torn instead of cut. Two ways to tear heavy (250-300 lb.) watercolor paper and get a "deckle-edged" look are:

1) Place the paper face down on a flat surface and score (but do not pierce) with an awl three or four times along the lines you wish to tear. Then bend back and forth at the scored line a few times. Then tear. This method will produce an attractive deckle-like edge.

2) Fold the paper along line where you wish to tear it, carefully moisten the fold, and, after the moisture has permeated the paper, tear it. The tear, which will follow the fold, will be very "deckle-like."

Collages on Watercolor Paper. — One of the advantages of making your collage directly on watercolor paper (*See Part III*) is that the mounting described in the previous paragraphs is unnecessary for collages made this way.

Whether made with clean margins or worked "edge-to-edge," collages on watercolor paper often look best when floated in the mat opening.

Sometimes it is nice to float a collage (whether made on matboard or watercolor paper) *off the surface* of its backing. This can be achieved by mounting it on an all-rag matboard spacer which is slightly smaller than the collage sheet before framing the work. Figure 9-2 shows how this is done.

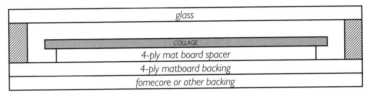

Figure 9-2: Floating a collage off the backing board without a mat.
The diagonally shaded pieces left & right represent
painted wood or "Framespace" spacers.

Glazing. — The proper glass or plastic sheeting is important for protecting collages. Because of the fugitive nature (fade-ability) of the inks and dyes which color many found objects, glazing which provides protection from ultraviolet light (the primary cause of fading) is desirable whenever possible.

It is important that the glass be kept away from the surface of the collage because a) when acrylic medium comes in contact with the glass the change in the index of refraction of the surfaces causes unsightly discoloration and b) If the collage is exposed to direct light the glass may get hot enough to melt the surface of the collage. For this reason double mats, 8-ply mats, or spacers[28] may be necessary depending on the thickness of the work and whether the mat covers the edge of the work or the work is floated.[29]

Collages on Canvas or Braced Wooden Panels. — Larger collages made on canvas, braced wooden panels or hollow-core doors[30] may be treated like paintings on panels for presentation purposes. Since many of these works will be framed unprotected by glazing, it is important to consider the varnishing options outlined in section VIII.

Thinking Ahead. — Whatever substrate you choose, it helps to have some idea of how you intend to mount, mat, and frame your collage before you start to work on it.

---

[28] See *Appendix: Glazing* Spacers are used to separate the glass from the artwork. Commonly they are made of painted balsa or other wood. There are also commercially manufactured plastic spacers sold under the brandname *Framespace.* Inquire from your framer.
[29] See *Appendix: Glazing*
[30] See Footnote 5 on Page 10.

PART X

ARCHIVAL CONCERNS

Because it is possible that giving too much attention to archival concerns can inhibit the creative process, I have purposely left this discussion to the last chapter of this book. One does well to keep in mind that such successful and famous artists as Picasso, Schwitters, and Cornell paid little or no attention to the archival qualities of the materials they used in making their collages. If you are satisfied to follow in their footsteps, you may wish to ignore this chapter altogether. But if you would avoid the embarrassment of having a collage fade or change color while you are still around to see it, you may wish to take note of the information presented here. — JT

Among the approaches to making collages which will last are these — 1. Choosing long-lasting materials and avoiding self destructive ones. 2. Preserving materials which are not naturally long-lasting. 3. Planning for change. 4. Preparing custom-made collage materials.

1. Identifying Long-lasting Materials. — Some materials commonly used by artists are naturally long-lasting but a number (including, surprisingly, some artists paints) are not. Since many of the "found" materials used by collage artists have unknown histories, the collage artist has a more difficult task than most in trying identifying materials which will be long-lasting. The guidelines which follow are general, and are to be used in conjunction with common sense since many exceptions exist.

Self-Destructive Materials. — Some materials available to collage artists change very rapidly. The paper on which modern newspapers are printed gets brown and brittle rapidly. Modern magazine pictures, color photo-copies, and most items printed on color inkjet printers will, if exposed to light, change color within a year or two as the red and yellow inks fade. Lines made with unpigmented markers, even those marked "permanent," have a relatively short life span. The artist who is intent on making lasting works will do well to find ways of preserving these materials or avoid using them altogether.

Papers. — Originally, all papers were made from cotton or linen rags or other natural fibers (this is where the terms "rag content" and "100% cotton" come from). The fibers of these materials are long and bind or "felt" together easily without additives. The resulting papers were, if the water was pure and the fibers devoid of additives, acid free and long lasting. Around the middle of the 19th century, new techniques were developed which allowed paper to be manufactured from wood pulp. Because the fibers in wood pulp are shorter, additives (sizing) are required to bind these fibers together into sheets of paper. These additives tend to be acidic and papers made with them tend to darken and get brittle. More recently (in the mid 1900s) some papermakers have added "buffering agents" to their premium wood-pulp papers in order to counteract the effects of the sizing. Such papers are sometimes described as "Neutral pH" papers.

While most contemporary papers are made from wood pulp, traditional cotton, linen and other natural fiber papermaking survives in the US, Europe, and Japan primarily to serve the needs of artists.[31]

---

[31] Lawyers also use 100% rag paper for writing wills and other documents which must last. A relatively inexpensive way to acquire all rag paper in to buy the 8 ½ x 11 or 8 ½ by 14 sheets that lawyers use for wills.

Inks. — Many materials of interest to collage artists are printed. Prior to the 20th century, most inks contained pigments and were long-lasting. Between 1900 and 1920, new processes were developed for making inks which were easier for printers to use. These inks are colored with dyes, not pigments, and fade relatively quickly when exposed to light.[32] Which type of ink (pigment or dye based) was used to print a particular image or text is not obvious to the naked eye (or even under a microscope) so it is wise to be aware of the dates of the materials you are using whenever possible.

PAPERS & INKS:
Papers from before 1850 are long-lasting.
Some newer papers (including some made for artists) are long-lasting.
Inks made before 1920 tend to resist fading better than newer ones.

---

2. Preserving Fugitive Materials. — Some materials which will fade, discolor, or become brittle may be treated to enhance their longevity. While coating fragile materials with acrylic medium will give them strength, it will not prevent them from fading or discoloring when exposed to light.

Neutralizing Acids in Paper and Fabrics. — Natural and acquired acids in paper and fabrics are one of the most common causes of fading, discoloration and deterioration. It is helpful to neutralize the acids if you wish to preserve paper and fabrics. One common way of neutralizing acids

---

[32] Most of us have seen calendars or posters which have turned blue as a result of exposure to light. This is because black and blue inks are more resistant to fading than red and yellow.

involves soaking the material you intend to use in an alkaline solution. You can prepare such a solution by dissolving a couple of Alka Seltzer tablets in a tray of carbonated water (club soda or seltzer). Allow the paper to thoroughly absorb the solution in the tray and then hang it up to dry.

For papers which cannot be soaked, spray products sold under the brand name "Wei T'o" can be sprayed on papers to deacidify them. "Wei T'o" comes in a variety of formulae and each has its advantages for certain types of materials.[33]

One of the most effective methods of inhibiting change in materials which are not lightfast is to coat the finished collage with a varnish which screens out ultraviolet light. This has already been discussed in Section VIII

3. Planning for Change. — When creating a collage, it may be wise to take into consideration the likelihood that certain materials may change with time and to plan for such an eventuality. A collage made with "change" in mind will retain its compositional integrity (balance) even if such changes take place.

The most important factor in this approach is avoiding using materials from different sources to balance each other.

Consider the pictures on the next page. If it were necessary to cut the stars out of questionable material, it would be important to make sure that all stars were cut from the *same* material.

---

[33] The Talas Catalog is a good source for information about Wei T'o (see Appendix)

Figure 10-1
"Stardreamer," a collage by the author

In the newly made collage all the stars are bright.

Figure 10-2

Some years have passed. Over time, exposure to light has faded the stars but since all the stars were cut out of the same material it has faded them *evenly* and the composition maintains its balance as shown here..

Figure 10-3

If some of the stars had been cut from one material and some from another, some might have faded while others did not. The result would have been the unbalanced composition pictured here.

4. Custom-Made Collage Materials. — Often it may be desirable to create custom made materials in order to be sure that your collage will be archivally sound.

Preparing Colored Papers. — Often it is difficult to find colored papers of the desired hue, value, or intensity. Also, most "ready-made" colored papers fade rapidly. The artist who wishes to make long-lasting collages which include colored papers will do well to follow in the footsteps of Matisse who, in his "Jazz" series and other "cutout" pieces, used papers which had been custom painted with permanent pigment paints in the colors of his choice.

One economical way to do this is to purchase the 100% cotton paper which lawyers use for preparing wills. Begin the process by mixing enough acrylic paint to give one side of each sheet *three coats* of the *same color* in order to completely obscure the white of the paper (the back of the sheet can remain white).[34] When painting papers lay them on a fresh sheet of newspaper when applying each coat and then move them to a drying rack to dry (see the section on "Coating Materials" in Part III). Allow each coat of paint to dry thoroughly before applying the next. When the final coat is dry, coat both sides of the sheets with gloss acrylic medium to prepare them for use.

Custom-Made Photocopied Materials. — A black and white photocopy can sometimes last longer than an original. One example of a situation where this can be useful is when you wish to include images or text from a newspaper in your collage. Since newspapers discolor (turn brown) rapidly, photocopying the desired text onto 100% cotton paper (*see Appendix*) can be helpful. Use a

---

[34] It helps to *slightly* thin the paint if you wish a smooth surface.

copier which uses toner rather than one of the newer ink-jet copiers as the ink from the ink-jet models may smear when the acrylic medium is being applied.[35] If the paper is too white one can tone or stain it after photocopying by dipping it in a dilute solution of paint, coffee, or other colorant.

Color Photocopies and Ink-Jet Output. — Color photocopies are not, in general, long lasting, even if they are made with a color copier that uses toner. With the exception of black toner (which contains carbon) the colors in toners are dye-based and fade very quickly when exposed to light. Ink–jet output is also subject to fading. Some manufacturers, recognizing this problem, are working to create archival quality ink-jet inks for use in color ink-jet printers. Keeping current with new developments is particularly important in this area.

Other Custom-Made Materials. — If you cannot find something you wish to include in your collage, consider making it. Use computers to create images and text. Cut or slice found objects to create interesting collage elements (thinly sawed cross-sections of old picture frames, for example). Block print or stamp papers or fabrics. Apply spray paint (taking proper safety precautions) to papers, fabrics, and three dimensional objects to make them the right color for your collage. Paint string or thread the color you want. Leave metal elements outside to rust if that look will enhance your collage. There are no limits to what you can make when you allow your imagination to explore freely.

---

[35] This is not true of all ink-jets (it depends on the ink) so you may wish to run your own tests.

Technique is but a small part of collage making. Choice and arrangement of materials, their size, shape, color, texture, images or text (if the materials contain them), and their personal and social implications, etc. will continue to be our primary concerns. Still, any working methods which make things easier and allow greater freedom for our creative energies and impulses are worth knowing.

— Jonathan Talbot

When I focus on making product, I lose the joy of the creative process, but when I focus on the creative process I not only enjoy it more but invariably the product is better.

— Wendy Hitchcock

APPENDIX

Acrylic Image Transfer Paper. — The ideal Acrylic Image Transfer Paper is clay-coated unvarnished paper of between 60 and 80 lbs. in weight which will not blister when exposed to the high heat of the fuser assembly in toner-based copy machines. A variety of commercially available (from printing paper supply houses) papers meet this description. At this time Talbot Arts is the only supplier of small quantities of Acrylic Image Transfer Paper for artists. *Sources: Talbot Arts, Warwick, NY 800-375-5133; Art Media, Portland, OR, 503-223-3724.*

Acrylic Mediums. — The techniques described in this monograph will work with a variety of different acrylic mediums. My choice is Polymer Medium (Gloss) #03510 made by Golden Artists Colors. *Sources: Your local art store or The Italian Art Store (NJ) 800-643-6440; New York Central Art Supply (New York) 212-473-7705; Cheap Joe's (NC) 800-227-2788; Art Media, Portland, OR, 503-223-3724.*

Adhesives. — No single technique or material is ideal in all circumstances. Each artist should be prepared to use whatever best serves her or his needs. A good source for a large variety of adhesives (including many not discussed in this book) is *Talas, 568 Broadway, New York, NY 10012, 212-219-0770 (E-mail: talas@sprynet.com).* Their catalog is a great source of information about adhesives.

Glazing / Ultraviolet Filtering. — Among the brands of glazing which filter out ultraviolet light are: Truevue Conservation Glass (advertised to provide 97% UV protection), available in both clear and non-glare; ICI Lucite Framing Acrylic with UVF is a plastic glazing material (like Plexiglas) , available in both clear and non-glare; Acrylite OP-3 AR (advertised to provide 98% UV protection), clear. *Sources: Your local framer or glass supply company or (for Acrylite) Light Impressions, Brea, CA 800-828-6216.*

Masking Tapes / Low-Tack. — Scotch 3M brand Safe-Release™ Masking Tape (#2070) and its translucent companion Scotch Removable Magic™ Tape (#811) are among the more useful tapes available to the artist. Their "low-tack" adhesives allow them to be safely removed even from delicate surfaces. The white paper-based

#2070 comes in ¾", 1", and 2" widths and is more resistant to the effects of water-based paints than #811. #811 is useful because you can see what is underneath it. *Sources: #2070 is available from paint stores and Home Depot. #811 is available in most stationery stores.*

Papers (100% Cotton for Photocopying). — There are a number of 100% cotton neutral pH papers which will easily pass through most copiers. Two of the more easy-to-obtain brands are Strathmore's *"Parchment Deed"* and Gilbert's *"Neutech 100% Cotton."*

PVA and other Adhesives. — Lineco Neutral pH Adhesive *(see Section IV)*: Lineco is a division of University Products, a company devoted to the manufacture of archival materials. Lineco Neutral pH PVA adhesive, the PVA Adhesive described in Section IV, is available in many art stores. University Products also sells Jade PVA adhesive #403N, Methyl Cellulose adhesive, Ethulose adhesive, and other archival adhesives each of which has its own special qualities. Perfect Paper Adhesive™ Gloss *(see Section IV)* is sold by USArtQuest, Inc. Another Neutral pH PVA Adhesive is GF#256UA made by Gluefast, Inc. of Neptune, NJ. This is the new version of GF#256 which was reportedly used by Romare Bearden. Also see "Adhesives" in this appendix. *Sources: Your local art store or University Products 800-628-1912 (ask for a catalog). USArtQuest, Inc., 7800 Ann Arbor Road, Grass Lake, MI 49240, Phone: 517-522-6228, www.usartquest.com. Gluefast, Inc., 3535 Rte 66, Building #1, Neptune, NJ 07753, phone: 732 918 4600 or 800 242 7318, e-mail: sales@gluefast.com, website: www.gluefast.com.*

Release Paper. — Release paper is paper impregnated and coated with silicone. Almost nothing sticks to release paper. Release paper is used on the back of self-adhesive postage stamps, mailing labels, and shelf-lining paper. Release paper comes both single and double sided. Since single-sided release paper can stick to your collage surface if inadvertently used upside down, it is better to purchase the double-sided variety. Release paper is available in sheets and rolls. *Sources: Talbot Arts, Warwick, NY 800-375-5133; Art Media, Portland, OR, 503-223-3724; Light Impressions, Brea, CA 800-828-6216.*

Ruling Pens. — Ruling Pens (also called drafting pens) are available in sets of drafting instruments which also contain ruling compasses and other drafting instruments (Ruling compasses are great for drawing arcs & circles). They can also be purchased singly. Since they are rarely used these days, they can often be found at flea markets and swap meets. Sources for used ruling pens also include: *Talbot Arts, Warwick, NY 800-375-5133*. Sources for new ruling pens include: *Talbot Arts, Warwick, NY 800-375-5133; Art Media, Portland, OR, 503-223-3724; or your local art store.*

Tacking Irons. — In selecting a tacking iron, one with a variable temperature control is desirable as single temperature irons may not be ideal for all materials. Four currently available variable temperature control tacking irons are the Black Baron Iron, the 21st Century Iron, and the Seal Selector II Iron, and the Hanger Nine Iron. The Black Baron Iron is solidly constructed with a flat bottom. Its temperature control is on top of the head. The 21st Century Iron retails for $44.95 and is lightweight and graceful with a gently rounded (at the tip) and pointed shoe. It's variable temperature control is mounted on the handle and is advertised to maintain an accurate temperature within 1.5 degrees. The Selector II Iron has a rounded, snub-nosed shoe with a curved tip and retails for approximately $75.00. Its temperature control is on top of the head. The Hangar Nine iron retails for about $20.00 and is solidly constructed with a curve upward at the point of the shoe. It's temperature control is on top of the head. My personal choice is a Hangar Nine iron because of the upward curve of the tip. I prefer a tacking iron with curved tip because it is more versatile. If you use a tacking iron with a flat bottom you must place the iron flat on the materials you are ironing and therefore heat an area equal to the entire area (and shape) of the bottom of the iron. If, however, you use an iron with a curved tip you can, by tilting the handle of the iron upwards, adjust the size of the area to which you apply heat. This is particularly useful when you want to iron down small elements or partially iron down large ones (see Part VI). As the heads of most irons are made of cast aluminum, one can "curve" the tip of a flat-bottomed iron with a belt or disc sander (use with caution... all power tools are dangerous) or a metal file and sandpaper. The illustrations below indicate the desired shape.. *Sources: Talbot Arts, Warwick, NY 800-375-5133; Art Media, Portland, OR, 503-223-3724.*

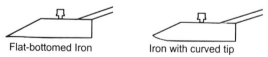

Flat-bottomed Iron   Iron with curved tip

Varnishes. — Varnishes containing ultraviolet filtering agents are recommended for protecting collages, especially those with modern "found" materials. Acrylic Varnishes are available in water soluble and mineral spirits soluble varieties. As has already been noted, it is important to use a varnish which can be removed by an agent different than that which will dissolve the medium used to create the work. The Golden Company makes both *water soluble polymer* and *mineral spirits soluble acrylic* varnishes which contain ultraviolet blocking agents and which can be removed without damaging works made with Golden Polymer Medium (Gloss). Both varieties are available in Gloss, Satin, and Matte finishes. In both cases Golden suggests that the varnishes be thinned before use as they are shipped "thick" to keep the filtering agents in suspension. The differences? Because of the nature of the ultraviolet filtering agents it is necessary to apply three coats of the water soluble polymer varnish to equal the ultraviolet protection of one coat of the mineral spirits acrylic varnish. Use of the mineral spirits varnish requires ventilation as the fumes are strong. *Sources: Your local art store or The Italian Art Store (NJ) 800-643-6440; New York Central Art Supply (New York City) 212-473-7705; Cheap Joe's (NC) 800-227-2788; Art Media, Portland, OR, 503-223-3724.*

BOOKS ABOUT COLLAGE & COLLAGE ARTISTS

Adventures with Collage,
Jan Beaney. Frederick Warne
& Co. / 1974

**The Art and Craft of
Collage**, Simon Larbalestier.
Chronicle Books / 1995

The Art of Assemblage,
William Seitz. NY,
MOMA / 1961

The Art of Collage, Gerald
Brommer. Worcester, MA,
Davis Publications / 1978

**The Art of Handmade
Paper and Collage**, Cheryl
Stevenson, Martingale & Co /
1998

The Art of Paper Collage,
Susan Pickering Rothamel
Sterling / 2000

**Romare Beardon: His Life
& Art**, Myron Schwartzman.
NY, Abrams / 1990

Georges Braque, Les Papiers
Colles, Douglas Cooper et.
al.. Centre Georges
Pompidou, Paris / 1982

Fritz Bultman : Collages,
Fritz Bultman, Eiland,
Windham, Firestone.
University of Georgia / 1997

Collage, Herta Wescher.
NY, Abrams / 1968

Collage, Francis Brow. NY,
Pitman Publishing / 1963.

Collage and Assemblage,
Trends & Techniques
Dona Meilach. NY,
Random House

Collage Art, Jennifer L.
Atkinson. Rockport / 1999

Collage Art, David Wild.
Rockport

**Collage, Assemblage, and
the Found Object**, Diane
Waldman. NY, Abrams /
1992

**Collage: A Complete Guide
For Artists**, Anne Brigadier.
NY, Watson-Guptill / 1972

Collage & Found Art,
Dona Meilach and Elvie Ten
Hoor. Reinhold / 1964

Collage Fundamentals.
Oscar Liebman. NY, Stravon
Ed. Press / 1979

The Collage Handbook,
John & Joan Digby. NY,
Thames and Hudson / 1985

**Collage: Pasted, Cut and
Torn Papers**, Florian Rodari.
NY, Rizzoli / 1988

**Collage: Personalities,
Concepts, Techniques**,
Harriet Janis. Philadelphia,
Chilton Co. / 1962

BOOKS ABOUT COLLAGE & COLLAGE ARTISTS (CONT.)

Collage Techniques, Gerald Brommer, Watson-Guptill / 1994

Collaged Photographs (Les Photographies Collages), Andre Villers. NY, Nahan Galleries / 1991

Joseph Cornell, Kynaston McShine. NY, MOMA / 1980

Utopia Parkway: The Life and Work of Joseph Cornell, Deborah Solomon. Farrar Straus & Giroux / 1997

Creative Collage for Crafters, Katherine Duncan Aimone, Lark Books / 2000

Creative Collage Techniques, Leland and Williams. F&W Pub.

In Defiance of Painting : Cubism, Futurism, and the Invention of Collage, Christine Poggi. Yale Univ. Press

Arthur Dove: The Years of Collage, Levitine et.al.. College Park, MD, Univ. of Maryland Art Gallery / 1967

Great Design Using Non-Traditional Materials, Sheree Clark & Wendy Lyons. North Light / 1996

Max Ernst Collages: The Invention of the Surrealist Universe, Werner Spies, NY Harry N. Abrams / 1988

Max Ernst, Dada and the Dawn of Surrealism, William A. Camfield, NY / 1993

Juan Gris, James Thrall Soby. NY, MOMA / 1958

History of Collage, Eddie Wolfram. NY, Macmillan / 1975

Cut with the Kitchen Knife, The Weimar Photomontages of **Hannah Hoch**, Maud Lavin, New Haven, Yale Univ. Press / 1993

Homo Ludens (**1 & 2**), Friedrich Meckseper. Germany/ 1984 & 1987

An Introduction to Mixed Media, Michael Wright. Dorling Kindersley / 1995

Jess, a Grand Collage, 1951-1993, Auping, Bertholf, Palmer, et.al. Buffalo Fine Arts Academy / 1993

Manual of Graphic Techniques, 1, Tom Porter and Bob Greenstreet. NY, Scribners / 1980

BOOKS ABOUT COLLAGE & COLLAGE ARTISTS (CONT.)

Henri Matisse: Paper Cut-Outs, Jack Cowart. St. Louis / Detroit, The St. Louis Art Museum & The Detroit Institute of Arts, 1977.

The Cut-Outs of Henri Matisse, John Elderfield. NY, Braziller / 1978

New Ways in Collage, Mary Mayer & Mary Webb. NY, Van Nostrand Reinhold / 1973

Paper Collage: Painted Paper Pictures, Christine McKechnie. / 1995

Pasted Paper: A Look at Canadian Collage, 1955-1965, Linda Milrod. Agnes Etherton Art Center, Kingston, Canada: 1979

Picasso and Braque / Pioneering Cubism, William Rubin, NY, MOMA / 1989

The Picasso Papers, Rosalind Krauss. Farrar / 1998

Principles of Collage, Brian French. London, Mills & Boon. / 1969

Realistic Collage: Step by Step, Brown, Metzger, Metzger. North Light Books / 1998

The Collages of Kurt Schwitters, D.Dietrich. Cambridge Univ. Press / 1995

Kurt Merz Schwitters: A Biography, Gwendolen Webster. Univ. of Wales / 1997

Kurt Schwitters, John Elderfield. NY, Thames & Hudson / 1985.

Kurt Schwitters, Werner Schmalenbach. NY, Abrams / 1970.

Alexis Smith, Richard Armstrong. NY, Whitney Museum, Rizzoli / 1992

Act Like Nothing's Wrong : The Montage Art of Winston Smith, Winston Smith, Dirk Dirksen, Last Gasp of San Francisco / 1994

Twelve American Masters of Collage, Andrew J. Crispo & Gene Baro. NY, Andrew Crispo Gallery / 1977

Un Semaine de Bonté, Max Ernst, NY, Dover / 1976

The Technique of Collage, Helen Hutton. Watson-Guptill, NY, 1968

Watercolor & Collage Workshop, Gerald Brommer, NY, Watson-Guptill / 1986

Internet Sites of Interest to Collage Artists

Artcolle: The site of Artcolle, an organization founded by Pierre Jean Varet which is devoted to documenting the art of collage worldwide. Text in French. http://users.aol.com/artcolle/index.htm

collageart.org: A site dedicated to the art of collage. Links to Collage Artists Sites, A Bibliography of Books on Collage, Presenters of Collage Workshops, Exhibition Opportunities for Collage Artists, and more. www.collageart.org

CollageGallery.com: A site created by artist David Turner. Collage and Assemblage artists can apply for internet shows here. www.collagegallery.com/index.html

Global Collage: The Collage Changes Every Thirty Seconds. An expanding and revolving exhibit of collages from around the world. You can submit your collages. www.globalcollage.com

International Museum of Collage, Assemblage, & Construction: Lots of collages and links to even more. www.post-dogmatist-arts.net/museum/collage/list.htm

Photomontage.com: An involved (and involving) collage-based site where the site itself is as much the art form as any of the work on it. www.photomontage.com

Jonathan Talbot's Studio: The website of the author. www.talbot1.com

E-Mail Lists of Interest to Collage Artists

Art_of_Collage: An e-mail list for the discussion and study of collage as an art. www.groups.yahoo.com/group/Art_of_Collage

AssemblageArtists: An e-mail list focusing on the art of assemblage. www.groups.yahoo.com/group/AssemblageArtists

collage: An e-mail list where you can communicate with other folks interested in collage. Created by Cecil Touchon. www.groups.yahoo.com/group/collage

collageartists: An e-mail list where you can communicate with other folks interested in collage. Created by Michelle Billett. www.groups.yahoo.com/group/collageartists

TalbotArtNet: An e-mail list focusing on techniques developed by the author. Created by Jennifer Jones. www.groups.yahoo.com/group/TalbotArtNet

INDEX

acrylic image transfers, 19
  alternate methods, 22
acrylic medium, 12, 27
  applying, 12
  gel, 22
  matte vs. gloss, 13
acrylic medium, 28
adhering elements, 7, 14
adhesives, 27
  alternatives to, 29
  chart of, 28
archival concerns, 37
Art Media (store), 46
assemblage, 1

beads of glue, 34
beveled edge, 33

canvas as a substrate, 11
Cheap Joe's (store), 46
circles (cutting), 25
clay coated unvarnished paper, 21
coating
  matboard, 9
  materials, 12
collage
  books about, 50
  defining, 1
  history of, 2
  internet sites about, 53
  potential of, 3
color copier, 21
color copies, fading of, 43
composition, 5, 7, 14
  creating, 7, 14
computers, 2, 43
construction, 1
Crazy Glue, 28
creating the composition, 7, 14

definition of collage, 1
drying racks, 12

elements (also see *materials*)
  metal, 29
  partially adhered, 24

elements (continued)
  plastic, 29
  three-dimensional, 29
Elmer's glue, 28
epoxy, 28

fading, 31
Fascinating Folds (store), 46
feathers, 16, 23
floating a collage in a mat, 35
flower petals, 16, 23
foil (hot stamping), 16, 25

gel acrylic medium, 22
gilding, 23
glazing, 33, 35, 46
Gluefast, Inc, 47
glue, see *adhesives*

hollow core doors, 10, 36
Home Depot, 47
hot glue gun, 28
hot stamping foil, 16, 25

inks, fading of, 39
injet output, 43
internet sites, 53
Italian Art Store, 46

joy, 45

Light Impressions, 46
linear elements, 26
lines (drawing), 26

margins (of watercolor paper), 10, 34
masking tape
  safe release, 10, 46
  low tack, 46
mat board
  as a Substrate, 8
  extra thick for framing, 33
materials
  adhering, 7
  coating, 12
  preparing, 6, 12

INDEX

matte medium, 13
matting, 33
metal leaf, 16, 23
model adhesive, 28
mounting, 33
museum board, 8

neutralizing acids, 39
New York Central Art Supply, 46

Pagemaker, 21
papers made from wood pulp, 38
papers made from cotton, 38
Perfect Paper Adhesive, 17
photocopies
    fading of color, 22, 43
    use in image transfer, 19, 22
    use in collages, 42, 43
planning for Change, 40, 42, 43
plastic kitchen wrap, 34
polyvinyl acetate adhesive, 17
potential of Collage, 3
poultry mesh, 12
pre-coated elements
    advantages of, 5
prepared panels, 10
preparing the materials, 6, 12
preparing the substrate, 6, 8
preserving fugitive materials, 39
PVA adhesive, 17, 28, 34, 47

Quark, 21

registration, 24
release paper, 7, 15
removal of elements, 23
reversed type, 21
rubber cement, 27, 28
ruling pen, 26, 47

safety, 3
self-destructive materials, 37
sewing, 29
silk, 16, 23

sources of supplies, 46
spacers, 36
storing prepared materials, 13
substrates
    preparing, 6, 8
    toning, 8
    types, 8

tacking iron, 7, 14, 48
    21st Century, 48
    Black Baron, 48
    modification, 48
    Selector II, 48
Talas (store), 46
Talbot Arts, 46
tearing paper, 34
thread, 16, 23
tissue paper, 16
toning the surface, 8
trimming, 33
Truevue conservation glass, 46

ultraviolet filtering agents, 48
ultraviolet light, 31, 32
University Products, 47
USArtQuest, 47

varnishing, 30
varnishes, 30, 31, 48
    mineral spirits soluble, 31, 48
    water soluble polymer, 31, 48

water-based inks, 21
watercolor paper, 9, 34
    as a Substrate, 9
waterproof ink, 19
weights, 34
wood pulp, 38
wooden panels, 36
wrinkling (elimination of), 5

Yes glue, 28

ACKNOWLEDGMENTS

This book has evolved, in part, as the result of a series of Collage Techniques and Creative Exploration workshops. I have been encouraged, informed and inspired by the participants in those workshops and a number of other individuals as well. Among those who deserve my special thanks are:

Marsha, Loren, and Garret Talbot
and
David Baquero, Laura Breitman, Gerald Brommer,
Nick Clemente, Diane Corson, Scott Fray,
Sophia Gevas, Claudine Hellmuth, Wendy Hitchcock,
Jean Houston, Geoffrey Howard, Arthur Lidov,
Roger Mudre, Joseph Rickards, Peggy Rubin,
Roderick Slater, and Andy Stasik,

— *Jonathan Talbot, 2001*

Photographs by Loren Talbot
Illustrations by the Author

Works by Jonathan Talbot have been exhibited at The National Academy and The Museum of Modern Art in New York, have represented the U.S. overseas in exhibitions sponsored by the State Department and the Smithsonian Institution, and are included in museum collections in the U.S. and Europe.